Word Games

Niels Grant, Jr.

 Lear Siegler, Inc./Fearon Publishers

Belmont, California

ISBN-0-8224-7485-9

Printed in the United States of America.

Contents

Introduction

The games in this book are designed to be played orally or used as vocabulary and spelling seatwork. Many of the games are progressive; that is, they move from simple, short sequences to longer, more complex ones. This enables every student to experience some measure of success and stimulates the more advanced students to greater achievement.

For the convenience of the teacher, lists of definitions and words are included for each game. These by no means represent all the words that are appropriate for a particular game. The teacher is encouraged to extend these lists and develop additional ones according to the needs of her classes. Many of the same words appear from game to game. This repetition of words and meanings has been done intentionally to help students learn new words and recognize them quickly in a new game.

For best effect, the teacher might want to include several different games in one assignment rather than using the games one at a time. Instructions are given for playing each game orally or using it as seatwork. If the teacher wishes to prepare a game sheet quickly, she may use the sample lists and merely substitute blanks

for the answers. For example, in the game "Juggling letters," list the original word and the definition of the new word followed by a blank:

horse	coastline	_____
cork	a stone	_____

The teacher may prefer to write out the game in sentence form:

"The letters of the word *horse* may be juggled to form a word that means *coastline*. The new word is _____."

Whether using the short form or the long, general directions for playing the game should always be included at the top of the game sheet.

No attempt has been made to prescribe how the games should be scored or whether they should be used for individual activities, for relay races and other team competition, or for enrichment or remedial work. This can best be determined by the individual teacher, and she should feel free to modify the games in any way that is appropriate for her particular students.

Juggling letters

In this game, the players are given one word and the definition of a new word. This new word can be formed by juggling the letters of the first word given. The game may be played orally or used as seatwork. In either case, these directions may be used: "The letters of the word (insert word) may be juggled to form a word that means (give definition). The new word is _____."
Some words to use when playing the game are listed below.

Word	Definition of New Word	New Word
ate	a liquid	tea
add	slang for a parent	dad
pot	a toy that spins	top
ram	part of the body	arm
woe	to be in debt	owe
art	a rodent	rat
how	a pronoun	who
tow	a number	two
end	home for lions	den
apt	to touch lightly	pat
kin	fluid for writing	ink
has	remains of fire	ash

Word	Definition of New Word	New Word
era	exists	are
pea	an animal	ape
now	to possess	own
tone	a short letter	note
race	tend; have feelings for	care
rate	rip; liquid from eye	tear
deal	a metal	lead
bead	in bed	abed
team	a kind of food	meat
pale	to jump	leap
mane	unkind; intend	mean
stun	almonds, pecans, etc.	nuts
bore	a kind of clothing	robe
doer	to have ridden	rode
tend	a depression	dent
dear	what you do to a book	read
post	a dot	spot
dies	surface forming border	side
ripe	dock	pier
cork	a stone	rock
felt	remaining	left
leap	the sound of a bell	peal
dial	set down	laid
lime	a measure of distance	mile
tops	pans	pots
trace	large wooden box	crate
timer	earn; deserve	merit
stone	musical qualities	tones
taste	to say; report	state
tired	attempted	tried
charm	to walk in time	march
miles	expression of happiness	smile
cares	frighten	scare
organ	sound of pain	groan
stage	openings in fences	gates
swore	opposite of better	worse
spear	extra	spare
horse	coastline	shore
rider	opposite of wetter	drier
livers	a metal	silver
secret	builds	erects

Word	Definition of New Word	New Word
regard	one who rates	grader
lamina	beast; creature	animal
aspire	laud; compliment	praise
canter	stupor	trance
course	origin; supplier	source
drawer	give in return for good deed	reward
dealer	one who guides	leader
verily	servant's uniform; horses for hire	livery
rename	one who means	meaner
tropes	placard; sign	poster

Add-a-letter

The purpose of this game is to form a new word by adding one letter at a time, using the given definitions as clues. The students start with a given letter and add a second letter to make a new word. The word must match the definition. Then a third letter is added to form a new word, and so on. Be sure to explain that occasionally the letters will have to be rearranged to make the new word. If the word he has just made proves to be incorrect when making the next word, the student will have to go back one step and find the correct word.

After giving general instructions, the game may be used in two ways: as a verbal assignment or as seatwork on ditto sheets. When used as a verbal assignment, the teacher should say: "We will begin with the letter _____. Now, add a letter that will form the word meaning _____. Next, add one letter that will form a word meaning _____," and so on.

If used as a dittoed assignment, follow this style:

Start with the letter _____ (give letter).
Add a letter to make a word meaning _____.   _____
Add a letter to make a word meaning _____.   _____
Add a letter to make a word meaning _____.   _____
Add a letter to make a word meaning _____.   _____

Here are sample letter and word combinations with appropriate definitions.

Definition	Word
start with	r
the second note of the scale	re
part of "to be"	are
to have feelings for	care
rich part of milk	cream
start with	t
a preposition	at
a rodent	rat
to evaluate	rate
a large wooden box	crate
start with	d
abbreviation for advertisement	ad
a boy	lad
to guide	lead
sharp part of a knife	blade
start with	t
a preposition	at
worn on the head	hat
idle talk	chat
capture	catch
start with	g
to leave; depart	go
self; intangible part of person	ego
leaves; departs	goes
type of large water bird	goose
start with	i
opposite of out	in
to succeed; be victorious	win
part of a single pair	twin
strong string	twine
start with	s
thus	so
male child	son
part of face	nose
loop in a rope	noose

Definition	Word
start with	*a*
part of "to be"	am
hold back water	dam
created	made
series of thoughts during sleep	dream
start with	*n*
negative word	no
another negative word	not
a musical sound	note
a rock	stone
start with	*t*
a preposition	to
decay	rot
to separate	sort
bad weather	storm
start with	*e*
personal pronoun	me
encountered	met
group of players	team
vapor from hot water	steam
start with	*d*
to accomplish; act	do
a small spot	dot
a froglike creature	toad
this 24-hour time period	today
start with	*a*
article	an
moving truck	van
instrument for telling wind direction	vane
type of bird	raven
start with	*o*
either	or
metal	ore
ripped	tore
market	store
start with	*l*
sixth note of the scale	la
a boy	lad
to guide	lead
postpone; slow down	delay

8

Definition	Word
start with	*h*
masculine pronoun	he
feminine pronoun	her
this place	here
good feeling; yell at game	cheer
start with	*a*
article	an
moved quickly; flowed	ran
past tense of ring	rang
big; wonderful	grand
start with	*a*
a part of "to be"	am
a small rug	mat
flesh food	meat
vapor from hot water	steam
start with	*i*
perhaps	if
part of a fish	fin
very good	fine
cutting tool	knife
start with	*a*
a preposition	at
label; a children's game	tag
opening in a fence	gate
big; wonderful	great
start with	*l*
sixth note of the scale	la
part of a race	lap
ashen; white-faced	pale
article of dinnerware	plate
start with	*h*
masculine pronoun	he
feminine pronoun	she
small building	shed
side of coin opposite of tails	heads
start with	*b*
to exist	be
wager	bet
to chew; nip	bite
group of Indians	tribe

Definition	Word
start with	*f*
fourth note of the scale	fa
distant	far
flat, wooden boat	raft
current of air	draft
start with	*w*
plural pronoun	we
damp	wet
gone away; departed	went
strong string	twine
start with	*f*
fourth note of the scale	fa
overweight	fat
destiny	fate
opposite of before	after
start with	*h*
sound of disbelief	ha
past tense of have	had
upper part of body; pate	head
shelter from sun	shade
start with	*o*
opposite of off	on
a number	one
a musical sound	tone
short letters	notes
start with	*i*
that thing	it
the end of something	tip
journey	trip
remove; take off; make bare	strip
start with	*l*
sixth note of the scale	la
to put or set down	lay
a woman	lady
postpone	delay
start with	*m*
slang for mother	ma
masculine person	man
hair on lion's neck	mane
intended	meant

10

Definition	Word
start with	*i*
exists	is
belongs to him	his
that particular item	this
article of clothing	shirt
start with	*m*
myself	me
encountered	met
hours, minutes, etc.	time
earn; deserve	merit
start with	*p*
a direction	up
to place	put
to sulk	pout
mouth of a teakettle	spout
start with	*r*
either	or
decay	rot
ripped	tore
not the same one	other
start with	*m*
personal pronoun	me
masculine people	men
belonging to me	mine
one who searches for gold	miner
start with	*n*
opposite of off	on
two thousand pounds	ton
short letter	note
musical qualities	tones
start with	*i*
that thing	it
be seated	sit
a particular object	this
used to lift heavy objects	hoist
start with	*n*
opposite of out	in
noise	din
obey	mind
dug up metals	mined

Definition	*Word*
start with	*w*
plural pronoun	we
sadness	woe
was wearing	wore
had written	wrote
start with	*d*
accomplish; act	do
female deer	doe
finished	done
type of bee; noise	drone
start with	*o*
sound of surprise	oh
garden tool	hoe
an opening	hole
where travelers stay	hotel
start with	*n*
an article	an
plus; also	and
ground up rock	sand
to be erect	stand
start with	*t*
a preposition	at
was seated	sat
a place to sit	seat
flavor	taste
start with	*u*
plural pronoun	us
solar body	sun
pecans, almonds, etc.	nuts
rotates	turns
start with	*r*
either	or
metal	ore
traveled on a horse	rode
direction; command	order
start with	*e*
masculine pronoun	he
an article	the
opposite of coldness	heat
used to make flour	wheat

12

Change-a-letter

This game involves matching a word to its definition and then changing one letter in the word to make a new word that matches a second definition. Explain to the class that it is often possible to make a new word by changing one letter in a word. Then give the definition of the first word, followed by the definition of the second word. Be sure the students understand that the two words must match the definitions and be different by only one letter.

Sample instructions might be: "Change one letter in a word meaning (give definition) to form a word that means (give definition)."

The examples that follow are arranged so that the words increase in difficulty and length.

Definition	Word	Definition	Word
exists	are	works produced by artists	art
negative word	not	decay	rot
was victorious	won	unit of weight	ton
storage place	bin	part of a fish	fin
sorrowful; unhappy	sad	not good	bad
the ocean	sea	to place	set
attempt	try	raise with a lever	pry
enemy	foe	low, wet clouds	fog

13

Definition	Word	Definition	Word
household pet	cat	was seated	sat
female deer	doe	small spot	dot
is able; permitted	may	speak	say
obtain	get	still; to come	yet
toss together, stir	mix	repair	fix
menu; cost of ride	fare	grow dimmer	fade
item that gives light	lamp	slanted floor	ramp
went; departed	gone	musical quality	tone
seek; search	hunt	damage; wound	hurt
drop or be dropped	fall	not succeed	fail
dispatch	send	pulverized rock	sand
belongs to me	mine	where money is made	mint
unit of time	hour	journey; guided visit	tour
a flower	rose	part of the face	nose
healthy; place for water	well	object that rings	bell
reduced price	sale	a story	tale
small vessel	boat	horned animal	goat
metal protector	grate	to rate	grade
form	shape	portion belonging to one	share
rich part of milk	cream	vision at night	dream
apply a liquid to walls	paint	lacking courage; to pass out	faint
flavor	taste	glue	paste
a number	eight	not dark	light
avoid; sidestep	dodge	inn; meeting place of an organization	lodge
oats, wheat, etc.	grain	part of the body	brain
raise into position	hoist	damp	moist
tip	point	connection	joint
surface	plane	to seed	plant
glass container	bottle	part of a war	battle
mend	repair	gave back (as money)	repaid
one, ten, etc.	number	wood from forest	lumber
cultivate land	harrow	slender; not broad	narrow
unopened; sealed	closed	a storage room	closet
part of automobile	fender	one who lends	lender
round wooden container	barrel	unfertile; plain	barren
part of the hand	finger	a spice	ginger
something put on mean dogs	muzzle	confuse; a mystery	puzzle
grocery store	market	one who grades	marker

14

Drop-a-letter

The purpose of this game is to supply a word that matches a given definition and then to form a new word with a new meaning by dropping one letter from the original word. Before starting, explain this to the students and warn them that, in most instances, it requires juggling the letters that are left.

For a dittoed assignment, use these directions: "Drop a letter from a word meaning (give definition) to get a word that means (give definition)."

In the examples that follow, the first section contains words made by dropping one letter; the second section contains words made by dropping two letters.

Definition	Word	Definition	Word
light brown	tan	an article	an
a light touch	pat	a preposition	at
a male child	son	a negative word	no
a metal	tin	opposite of out	in
a feminine pronoun	she/her	a masculine pronoun	he
ripped	tore	metal	ore
to grade	rate	a rodent	rat
tend; have feelings for	care	exists	are
departed; left	gone	a number	one

Definition	Word	Definition	Word
part of a pair	twin	victorious	win
a flesh food	meat	encountered	met
what a bell did	rang	remnant of cloth	rag
very good	fine	part of a fish	fin
opening in a fence	gate	had eaten	ate
a small building	shed	feminine pronoun	she
journey	trip	tear	rip
ripped	tore	decay	rot
short letter	note	two thousand pounds	ton
place to sit	seat	ocean	sea
to grade	rate	a liquid	tea
male royalty	king	writing material	ink
vessel	ship	part of the body	hip
trim; clean	neat	had eaten	ate
hours, minutes, etc.	time	encountered	met
snare; catch	trap	light touch	pat
rich part of milk	cream	tend; have feelings for	care
large wooden box	crate	to grade	rate
idea; vision at night	dream	precious; word of love	dear
a rock	stone	short letter	note
bad weather	storm	decays	rots
this 24-hour period	today	a froglike creature	toad
grocery; market	store	ripped	tore
postpone	delay	guide	lead
happiness; school yell	cheer	this place	here
huge; excellent	grand	what the bell did	rang
vapor from hot water	steam	a flesh food	meat
cutting tool	knife	very good	fine
excellent; huge	great	opening in a fence	gate
to earn	merit	hours, minutes, etc.	time
mode of transportation	train	type of weather	rain
a lid	cover	on top	over
large wooden box	crate	to rip; moisture from eyes	tear
reflection; picture	image	contest; recreational device	game
a shelf	ledge	border; rim	edge
verify	prove	wander	rove
promise	pledge	a shelf	ledge
oil product	grease	strike out; remove	erase
•		• •	
a plot	plan	an article	an
trim; clean	neat	a preposition	at

Definition	Word	Definition	Word
hours, seconds, etc.	time	a personal pronoun	me
snare	trap	a preposition	at
the earth; dirt	soil	thus	so
healthy; place to get water	well	pronoun	we
not closed	open	negative word	no
hours, seconds, etc.	time	pronoun	it, me
part of the ear	lobe	to exist	be
trim; clean	neat	an article	an
a dark color	brown	at this time	now
let; permit	allow	entire	all
large wooden box	crate	rodent	rat
place to go in	entry	a number	ten
ledge	shelf	a small creature; fairy	elf
to sow seed	plant	part of a race	lap
ordinary; unadorned	plain	fastening device	pin
evidence	proof	in favor of; preposition	for
moan	groan	loped; scurried	ran
border	frame	to deface	mar
where flowers grow	garden	pull along behind	drag
a brightly colored bird often kept as a pet	parrot	snare	trap
give	donate	finished	done
come back	return	rotate; veer	turn
three-legged stand	tripod	journey	trip
keeper; protector	warden	term of endearment	dear
promise	pledge	border; rim	edge
safe; tie down	secure	certain	sure
greeting	salute	seasoning	salt
come back	return	smallest (as animal)	runt
define; make clear	explain	ordinary; unadorned	plain
get ready	prepare	what we write on	paper
cargo	freight	a number	eight
tender; breakable	fragile	unhealthy; fragile	frail
odd	strange	stove; degree	range
made safe	secured	makes well	cures
to run (as a machine)	operate	musical play	opera
rebel; argue against	protest	grocery; market	store
of the soil	earthen	part of the body (organ)	heart
a picture	drawing	twist	wring
force in or upon	intrude	tendency	trend

Drop-a-letter (categories)

This game is similar to "Drop-a-letter" except that the words are organized by categories. Give the students a definition of a word, and tell them that by dropping one letter in the word they can make a new word that will fit into a certain category (such as trees, birds, etc.). Explain that the letter may be dropped from the beginning, middle, or end of the word.

If you want to play the game verbally, you may wish to use these instructions: "Drop a letter from a word meaning (give definition) to get a word that belongs in the (give category) category."

For a dittoed assignment, include some general directions at the top of the sheet and then set the page up like this:

Category: _____

(Give definition) Word _____   Category Word _____

Definition	Word	Category Word
CATEGORY: TREES		
well-liked	popular	poplar
let stand in water	soak	oak
steering wheel of ship	helm	elm

18

Definition	Word	Category Word
CATEGORY: TREES — *continued*		
to crush	mash	ash
backbone	spine	pine
sacred song or poem	psalm	palm
CATEGORY: WEIGHTS AND MEASURES		
leap upon	pounce	ounce
kind of bird (canary-like)	finch	inch
musical quality	tone	ton
a play; serious story	drama	dram
impress letters on	print	pint
small dot	speck	peck
CATEGORY: BODY PARTS		
group of ships	fleet	feet
slides out of place	slips	lips
injury; damage	harm	arm
listens; heeds	hears	ears
ripped	tore	toe
to glisten	shine	shin
part of fireplace	hearth	heart
splinter	sliver	liver
listen	hear	ear
looped rope	noose	nose
cultivated land	farm	arm
bend down	kneel	knee
CATEGORY: ANIMALS AND MAMMALS		
hair on face	beard	bear
ribbon; adhesive	tape	ape
a hood	cowl	cow
small wagon	cart	cat
to rob	steal	seal
to act self-satisfied	gloat	goat
CATEGORY: BIRDS		
noise made by dog	howl	owl
cowardly	craven	raven
recoil; wince	flinch	finch
kind of small dog	beagle	eagle
large group of people	crowd	crow
feel sorrow; rue	regret	egret

19

Definition	Word	Category Word
CATEGORY: FOOD		
intended	meant	meat
mountain tops	peaks	peas
cost	price	rice
part of a door	jamb	jam
heap	pile	pie
hoax; fake	sham	ham
CATEGORY: FRUIT		
give a sermon	preach	peach
lance; sword	spear	pear
trimmed trees	pruned	prune
cover with spots	dapple	apple
slippery substance	slime	lime
CATEGORY: PRONOUNS		
small building	shed	she
unit of time	hour	our
group of animals	herd	her
topic; composition	theme	them
particular object	this	his
bitter; not sweet	sour	our
CATEGORY: NUMBERS		
made from wheat	flour	four
finished	done	one
poundage	weight	eight
care for	tend	ten
needs water	thirsty	thirty
very heavy	weighty	eighty

Backward words

In this game, the word that matches the first definition can be spelled backward to produce a word that matches the second definition. The game may be played orally with the teacher giving the definitions and the students supplying the words.

If you want to use the game as seatwork, ditto off game sheets with these directions: "Spell a word that means (give definition) backwards and it will produce a word that means (give meaning)."

As an alternate, give general instructions and then list the definitions in two columns with a blank following each definition:

clothing _____   boast _____

Sample definitions and words are listed below.

Definition	Word	Definition	Word
preposition	on	negative word	no
a part of "to be"	am	slang for mother	ma
thus	so	bone	os
a meshed material	net	a number	ten
male sheep	ram	stain; deface	mar
uncooked	raw	conflict between nations	war
a negative word	not	two thousand pounds	ton

21

Definition	Word	Definition	Word
dampness in the morning	dew	marry	wed
four-legged pet	dog	supreme being; deity	God
once lived	was	a cutting tool; observed	saw
hang down in the middle	sag	fuel for engines	gas
angry; insane	mad	used to hold back water	dam
a point	tip	hole	pit
equal	par	knock; talk	rap
to snare	trap	portion; to separate	part
to sketch	draw	to guard; fend off	ward
an antlered animal	deer	long, slender grass	reed
English streetcar	tram	market place	mart
break suddenly	snap	pots	pans
sharp taste	tang	small flying insect	gnat
to rob	loot	instrument	tool
pace; part of stairway	step	household animals	pets
five-pronged shape	star	rodents	rats
game played on a course	golf	to beat	flog
wild animal	wolf	move along (as water)	flow
rise and fall of ocean	tide	to correct printed work	edit
to exist	live	bad; sinful	evil
hang onto; maintain	keep	look secretively	peek
part of a ship	keel	kind of green vegetable	leek
clothing	garb	boast	brag
to give out (as an odor)	emit	hours, seconds, etc.	time
double purpose	dual	to praise	laud
plain; dull	drab	a poet	bard
dried hay	straw	growths on the skin	warts
used to pry	lever	boisterous; happy	revel
kind of boat	sloop	small bodies of water	pools
one who keeps time	timer	return; send in	remit
bobbin; thread holder	spool	circles in string or rope	loops
intelligent	smart	English streetcars	trams
drive back; offend	repel	diseased person	leper
strata; part of cake	layer	send on	relay
argue; prove wrong	rebut	parts of plants (roots)	tuber
removes skin from fruit	peels	suspended consciousness	sleep
existed	lived	satan	devil
part of a dresser	drawer	gift for a good deed	reward
change instruments	retool	one who robs	looter
did something in return	repaid	clothing for baby	diaper

Connections

The teacher gives the students the first letter, or letters, of a word, the definition of a root word, and the definition of the final, complete word. The student must then figure out the root word and the final word. Either of these directions can be given, depending on the order you want to follow.

"Add (give letter[s]) to a word meaning (give definition) to make a word meaning (give definition)."

"A word meaning (give definition) is made by adding the letter(s) (give letter[s]) to a word meaning (give definition)." The columns would be in this order: Definition of New Word, New Word, Letter, Definition of Root Word, Root Word.

When using the game as seatwork, you may wish to set up your dittoed assignment page like this:

Definition of New Word	New Word	Letter(s)	Definition of Root Word	Root Word

Letter(s)	Definition	Root Word	Definition of New Word	New Word
b	a preposition	in	storage place	bin
f	a preposition	at	overweight	fat
t	an article	an	a light color	tan

Letter(s)	Definition	Root Word	Definition of New Word	New Word
s	that thing	it	be seated	sit
b	advertisement	ad	not good	bad
r	a preposition	at	rodent	rat
a	leave; depart	go	the past	ago
j	to exist	am	jelly	jam
s	a preposition	on	male child	son
t	a preposition	in	a metal	tin
b	exist	are	plain; unadorned	bare
t	monkeylike animal	ape	a ribbon	tape
r	exist	are	unusual	rare
t	knock; talk	rap	snare	trap
s	lubricate	oil	earth	soil
s	a conjunction	and	ground up rock	sand
w	sick	ill	determination	will
o	place for animals	pen	unclosed	open
h	opposite of young	old	grasp; keep	hold
l	a conjunction	and	ground	land
p	path	lane	surface; make smooth	plane
p	meshed material	lace	to put; location	place
t	contest	race	to copy	trace
t	this place	here	that place	there
s	ripped	tore	market	store
l	rim; border	edge	protrusion; shelf	ledge
p	wandered	rove	verify	prove
s	level; the same	even	a number	seven
g	to grade	rate	rasp	grate
s	small nail	tack	pile	stack
b	unit of weight	ounce	jostle	bounce
g	say; speak	utter	waterway	gutter
h	not younger	older	container	holder
s	article of furniture	table	secure; place for horse	stable
w	a number	eight	ounces, pounds, etc.	weight
k	opposite of day	night	royalty	knight
g	spear	lance	quick look	glance
g	circular	round	land; pulverized	ground
s	vote into office	elect	choose	select

• • •

| ho | pronoun | me | residence | home |
| me | article | an | intend; ornery | mean |

24

Letter(s)	Definition	Root Word	Definition of New Word	New Word
do	either	or	opening in wall	door
ne	preposition	at	tidy; clean	neat
sp	preposition	in	rotate; turn around	spin
li	preposition	on	king of beasts	lion
lo	exist	be	part of the ear	lobe
sk	preposition	in	body covering	skin
ti	personal pronoun	me	minutes, hours, etc.	time
br	possess	own	a dark color	brown
al	not high	low	let; permit	allow
cr	had eaten	ate	large wooden box	crate
en	attempt	try	place of entrance	entry
ha	a small quantity	bit	automatic act	habit
sh	a small creature	elf	ledge	shelf
st	uncooked	raw	used for drinking	straw
im	period of time	age	picture; reflection	image
st	a conjunction	and	be erect	stand
pl	small insect	ant	to sow	plant
pl	border	edge	promise	pledge
sa	musical instrument	lute	greet	salute
re	rotate; veer	turn	come back	return
st	scratch	itch	sew	stitch
gr	comfort	ease	lubricate	grease
to	custody	ward	leading to	toward
re	make; mold	form	make again; correct	reform
sh	place to skate	rink	grow smaller	shrink
se	mend; make well	cure	safe	secure
un	just; carnival	fair	unjust	unfair
ex	unadorned	plain	make clear	explain
fr	a number	eight	cargo	freight
en	huge	large	make bigger	enlarge
fr	nimble; balanced	agile	breaks easily	fragile
st	stove	range	odd; peculiar	strange
se	made well	cured	made safe; got	secured
ex	enough	ample	model; sample	example
en	repeated song	chant	thrill; interest	enchant
de	smoothed off	filed	marred; deface	defiled
		• • •	•	
pla	preposition	in	unadorned	plain
sed	an article	an	type of automobile	sedan

Letter(s)	Definition	Root Word	Definition of New Word	New Word
wom	an article	an	female	woman
pro	preposition	of	evidence; verification	proof
gro	an article	an	moaning sound	groan
tra	preposition	in	mode of transportation	train
gle	exists	am	glisten; shine	gleam
fra	personal pronoun	me	border	frame
ene	pronoun	my	foe	enemy
dra	slang for mother	ma	a play	drama
gar	where lions live	den	where flowers grow	garden
par	decay	rot	colored bird	parrot
don	had eaten	ate	give	donate
ret	large vase	urn	come back	return
sad	home for lions	den	make unhappy	sadden
tri	container for peas	pod	three-legged stand	tripod
war	home for lions	den	guard; protector	warden
ret	anger	ire	stop; go to sleep	retire
pil	not high	low	cushion	pillow
nec	black, sticky substance	tar	sweet liquid	nectar
dra	part of a bird	wing	etching; done in art	drawing
ope	grade	rate	run	operate
exa	belongs to me	mine	look over; test	examine
pro	examination	test	argue against	protest
mar	royal man	king	writing on; grading	marking
int	impolite	rude	enter impolitely	intrude
lei	positive; certain	sure	spare time	leisure
wor	vessel	ship	adore	worship
pre	peel; take rind off	pare	make ready	prepare
ear	that time	then	of the soil	earthen
fra	allow; give to	grant	nice aroma	fragrant
res	mode of transportation	train	hold back	restrain
tri	a direction	angle	three-sided form	triangle
env	run away to marry	elope	folder for letter	envelope
dis	lid	cover	find; unearth	discover
dis	work out; prove	solve	fall apart; melt	dissolve
det	was ill	ailed	worked out clearly	detailed
clo	an object	thing	wearing apparel	clothing
col	run out; expire	lapse	fall apart; fall down	collapse
mat	a long lock of hair	tress	cushion for a bed	mattress

26

Word sandwich

Explain that there is often a small word inside a big word. Tell the class that they are going to play a game in which they will put a small word between two letters to form a new word.

The game may be played verbally or dittoed for seatwork. In either case, you may wish to use the following directions: "When a word meaning (give definition) is put between the letters (give letters), it forms a word meaning (give definition)."

Definition	Root Word	Letters	Definition of New Word	New Word
a negative word	no	k - - t	measure of ship's speed	knot
opposite of out	in	m - - t	where money is made	mint
part of "to be"	am	d - - p	wet	damp
indefinite article	an	b - - k	where money is kept	bank
personal pronoun	me	a - - n	prayer ending	amen
indefinite article	an	t - - k	vehicle for war	tank
opposite of off	on	p - - d	small body of water	pond
a negative word	no	k - - w	aware of	know

Definition	Root Word	Letters	Definition of New Word	New Word
an alternative	or	b - - e	drill	bore
plural pronoun	we	a - - d	agog; in wonderment	awed
an alternative	or	p - - k	kind of meat	pork
opposite of out	in	l - - e	a row	line
part of "to be"	is	l - - t	roster; enumeration	list
indefinite article	an	v - - e	tells direction of wind	vane
indefinite article	an	w - - t	desire; need	want
plural pronoun	us	f - - s	ado; fret	fuss
opposite of out	in	z - - c	metallic element	zinc
an alternative	or	c - - e	center	core
indefinite article	an	g - - g	group	gang
that one	it	b - - e	chew; nip	bite
a preposition	of	l - - t	upper floor of barn	loft
like	as	p - - s	go by	pass
player in a game (as tag)	it	p - - y	feel sorry for	pity
exist	be	a - - d	ready for sleep	abed
what we breathe	air	f - - - y	a make-believe person	fairy
female sheep	ewe	f - - - r	less than	fewer
propel a boat	row	c - - - d	large group of people	crowd
what we breathe	air	d - - - y	farm where milk is produced	dairy
be in debt	owe	l - - - r	not as high as	lower
organ of hearing	ear	b - - - d	growth of hair on face	beard
positive vote	aye	p - - - r	one who makes payment	payer
a primate	ape	p - - - r	writing material	paper
edge	rim	g - - - e	dirt; filth	grime
colored by sun	tan	s - - - d	to be erect	stand
anger	ire	t - - - d	weary	tired
deliver a blow	hit	w - - - e	without color; opposite of black	white
be in debt	owe	t - - - r	spire	tower
male sheep	ram	t - - - p	walk heavily; hobo	tramp

28

Definition	Root Word	Letters	Definition of New Word	New Word
droop in middle	sag	u - - - e	a customary procedure	usage
a beverage	ale	v - - - t	male servant	valet
be in debt	owe	v - - - l	opposite of consonant	vowel
organ of hearing	ear	w - - - y	tired	weary
belonging to him	his	w - - - k	brush lightly	whisk
equal; accepted standard	par	s - - - e	extra	spare
cover for pan	lid	g - - - e	slide, coast	glide
illuminated	lit	e - - - e	special group	elite
belonging to us	our	c - - - t	where trials are held	court
walked hurriedly	ran	c - - - k	mean person; used to start a motor	crank
rodent	rat	c - - - e	large wooden box	crate
posterior; the back	rear	d - - - - y	dull; lifeless	dreary
small path	lane	p - - - - t	a heavenly body	planet
used to tie shoe	lace	p - - - - d	to have put something somewhere	placed
one who helps	aide	m - - - - n	young woman	maiden
moving structure made of logs	raft	d - - - - y	in a breeze	drafty
run in competition	race	b - - - - d	made stronger; supported	braced
misplace	lose	c - - - - d	unopened; sealed	closed
a trumpet	horn	t - - - - y	covered with stickers	thorny
to peel	pare	s - - - - d	saved	spared
belonging to us	ours	c - - - - e	direction; way	course
rim, border	edge	l - - - - r	record; accounts	ledger

Key words

Before playing this game, explain that the same word may be formed in several larger words and give some examples. Warn the class that the key word may not always be pronounced the same when it is part of another word (one−bone−money). Begin the game by giving the key word, e.g., *air*, and then the definitions. The students should supply words that match the definitions.

Definition	*Word*
KEY WORD: ASK	
covering for the face	mask
a chore	task
a round container	cask
KEY WORD: ARE	
naked	bare
tend; have feelings for	care
female horse	mare
KEY WORD: OUT	
a fight	bout
sulk	pout
awkward, clowning person	lout

30

Definition	Word
KEY WORD: AIL	
greet; frozen rain	hail
go to sea	sail
not succeed	fail
KEY WORD: ACE	
meshed fabric	lace
walk back and forth	pace
part of the head	face
KEY WORD: LED	
lost blood	bled
ran away	fled
toboggan	sled
KEY WORD: INK	
type of fur	mink
place to skate	rink
submerge	sink
KEY WORD: OIL	
wind up	coil
earth	soil
seethe, bubble	boil
KEY WORD: ALL	
drop; season of year	fall
high	tall
round toy	ball
KEY WORD: AIR	
honest	fair
a seat	chair
defeat; sorrow	despair
mend	repair
home of a lion	lair
KEY WORD: MAR	
to make a sign on; grade	mark
of the sea	marine
grocery store	market
rules of a language	grammar
parade; walk in step	march

Definition	*Word*

KEY WORD: OLD

keep; maintain	hold
a precious metal	gold
not as hot as	colder
to correct someone angrily or sharply	scold
open up; straighten out	unfold
brave; strong	bold
related; narrated	told

KEY WORD: ONE

part of the skeleton	bone
fair; trustworthy	honest
glistened; shined	shone
single; by oneself	alone
nickles, dimes, etc.	money
seat for a king	throne
not any	none

KEY WORD: ATE

destiny	fate
turn in circles	rotate
tell; narrate	relate
came after; not as early as	later
fill with air	inflate
used for gliding on ice	skate

KEY WORD: MAN

a living person	human
way of acting; proper actions	manners
insist, order	demand
female person	woman
order	command
hair on horse or lion	mane

KEY WORD: LAD

part of a meal	salad
used for climbing	ladder
happy; pleased	glad
spoon for serving soup, etc.	ladle
metal on knife	blade
well-mannered woman	lady

32

Definition	*Word*

KEY WORD: RAT

to grade	rate
run (as a machine)	operate
toy for baby	rattle
anger; rage	wrath
rasp; metal protector over hole	grate
to create power	generate

KEY WORD: RAN

stove; a row of mountains	range
big; wonderful	grand
position in army; to rate	rank
mark on cattle	brand
move to another place	transfer
one part of a piece of rope or yarn	strand

KEY WORD: EAR

the land; our planet	earth
go out of sight	disappear
chief part of the human body	heart
fright	fear
dull; cheerless	dreary
promise	swear

KEY WORD: ORE

to drill	bore
put away for later use	stored
where trees grow	forest
points (as in a game)	score
take the center out	core
edge of the sea	shore

KEY WORD: OUR

not sweet	sour
way; path over which something moves	course
unit of time	hour
used in baking; made from wheat	flour
trip	journey
a planned trip	tour
origin; where something starts	source

Definition	*Word*

KEY WORD: END

rely on	depend
last; tolerate	endure
one who loans	lender
twist	bend
part of automobile	fender
slim	slender

KEY WORD: PEN

used for writing	pencil
rely on	depend
grow deeper	deepen
unclosed	open
pay money out	spend
waiting; not yet decided	pending

KEY WORD: OWE

a spire	tower
rose, pansy, etc.	flower
was in debt	owed
ran (as water)	flowed
light rain	shower

KEY WORD: EAT

loss of a contest	defeat
trim, clean	neat
devoured	eaten
lost; was defeated	beaten
rain, sunshine, etc.	weather

KEY WORD: ART

small wagon	cart
an object; short, written item	article
opposite of arrival	departure
unit of liquid measure	quart
map	chart

KEY WORD: CAN

taper; wax item used for light	candle
a kind of nut	pecan
to look across	scan
kind of (yellow) bird	canary
spectacular gossip; disgrace	scandal
empty	vacant

Definition	_Word_
KEY WORD: LET	
note sent through the mail; part of alphabet	letter
small bay	inlet
a bright color	scarlet
leave out; take out	delete
kind of hammer	mallet
green vegetable	lettuce
KEY WORD: DEN	
happening unexpectedly	sudden
move in from margin	indent
thick	dense
pertaining to teeth	dental
crash; unintended event	accident
KEY WORD: CAR	
a bright color	scarlet
rug	carpet
frighten	scare
mark left by wound	scar
orange-colored vegetable	carrot
wheeled vehicle	carriage
KEY WORD: MEN	
said at end of a prayer	amen
of the mind	mental
material used in building	cement
substance; part of something	element
repair	mend
huge, large	immense
KEY WORD: HER	
plume	feather
that place	there
famous person, loved and respected	hero
of the south	southern
group of animals	herd
not at any place	nowhere
KEY WORD: RAIN	
rye, oats, etc.	grain
part of the body	brain
to run off; empty	drain

Definition	*Word*
<small>KEY WORD:</small> RATE	
large wooden box	crate
rasp; metal protector	grate
furious; angry	irate
<small>KEY WORD:</small> EVER	
to cut	sever
pry; tool for prying	lever
not at any time	never
<small>KEY WORD:</small> OVER	
remain over a place	hover
lid	cover
one who adores	lover
<small>KEY WORD:</small> RAFT	
art	craft
cold air	draft
corruption	graft
<small>KEY WORD:</small> RANK	
tool for starting engine	crank
sipped	drank
honest, open	frank
<small>KEY WORD:</small> RACE	
copy	trace
support; make stronger	brace
prayer before meals	grace
<small>KEY WORD:</small> EASE	
stop	cease
to rent or hire	lease
pester	tease
<small>KEY WORD:</small> EAST	
used to make dough rise	yeast
banquet	feast
animal	beast
<small>KEY WORD:</small> INCH	
to make secure	cinch
type of bird	finch
squeeze between finger and thumb	pinch

Rhymes

Briefly discuss rhymes and verse to be sure the students are familiar with them. Then explain that in this word game, the students must supply a word that matches the definition and that rhymes with the last word of the first sentence. Once the children understand the purpose of the game, it may be played orally or used for seatwork.

Rhyme	*Word*
A word that rhymes with *that* Is a household pet called a _____.	cat
A word that rhymes with *dog* Is a piece of wood called a _____.	log
A word that rhymes with *true* Is a number that is _____.	two
A word that rhymes with *shout* Is the opposite of in, so is _____.	out
A word that rhymes with *flag* Is one meaning to fall behind, to _____.	lag
A word that rhymes with *boy* Is a mood of happiness called _____.	joy

Rhyme	Word
A word that rhymes with *task* Means to question, or to _____.	ask
A word that rhymes with *bear* Is what we breathe, the _____.	air
A word that rhymes with *fun* Is a weapon called a _____.	gun
A word that rhymes with *shed* Is a place to sleep called a _____.	bed
A word that rhymes with *sky* Is an organ of sight, the _____.	eye
A word that rhymes with *leg* Means to plead, or to _____.	beg
A word that rhymes with *sky* Is an insect called a _____.	fly
A word that rhymes with *door* Is a conflict called a _____.	war
A word that rhymes with *flower* Is a pronoun; it is _____.	our
A word that rhymes with *shoe* Is a pronoun; it is _____.	you
A word that rhymes with *four* Is an opening called a _____.	door
A word that rhymes with *shed* Is a part of the body called the _____.	head
A word that rhymes with *pledge* Is a border, or the _____.	edge
A word that rhymes with *drive* Is a number that is _____.	five
A word that rhymes with *park* Is a bird called the _____.	lark
A word that rhymes with *best* Is a direction; it is the _____.	west
A word that rhymes with *true* Is a color; it is _____.	blue
A word that rhymes with *pure* Means to be certain, to be _____.	sure

Rhyme	Word
A word that rhymes with *date* Is the part of a fence called the _____.	gate
A word that rhymes with *should* Is a building material called _____.	wood
A word that rhymes with *snap* Is a snare, or a _____.	trap
A word that rhymes with *bad* Means to be happy, to be _____.	glad
A word that rhymes with *said* Means to run away, to have _____.	fled
A word that rhymes with *care* Means to put on, or to _____.	wear
A word that rhymes with *five* Is a home for bees, a _____.	hive
A word that rhymes with *flower* Is a unit of time, an _____.	hour
A word that rhymes with *stem* Is a pronoun; it is _____.	them
A word that rhymes with *think* Is a place to skate, a _____.	rink
A word that rhymes with *pledge* Is a shelf called a _____.	ledge
A word that rhymes with *yellow* Is a greeting, to say _____.	hello
A word that rhymes with *seem* Is the rich part of milk, the _____.	cream
A word that rhymes with *great* Is a wooden box, a _____.	crate
A word that rhymes with *freight* Is a number; it is _____.	eight
A word that rhymes with *barge* Describes a size as _____.	large
A word that rhymes with *ink* Means to concentrate, to _____.	think
A word that rhymes with *salute* Is a kind of food called _____.	fruit

Rhyme	Word
A word that rhymes with *crane* Is a way to travel, to go by _____.	train
A word that rhymes with *slate* Means to be large, wonderful, or _____.	great
A word that rhymes with *rare* Describes something extra, a _____.	spare
A word that rhymes with *team* Means to have a vision, to have a _____.	dream
A word that rhymes with *choke* Is what rises from a fire; it's _____.	smoke
A word that rhymes with *rhyme* Means to scale a mountain, to _____.	climb
A word that rhymes with *merry* Is the place where cows are kept, the _____.	dairy
A word that rhymes with *bare* Means to make a promise, to _____.	swear
A word that rhymes with *aloud* Means to feel pride, to be _____.	proud
A word that rhymes with *funny* Describes coins and currency; it's _____.	money
A word that rhymes with *ease* Means to satisfy, to _____.	please
A word that rhymes with *bread* Is a string used to sew, it's called _____.	thread
A word that rhymes with *fool* Tells where you go to learn, the _____.	school
A word that rhymes with *pickle* Is a unit of money, the _____.	nickle
A word that rhymes with *gate* Means to give, to _____.	donate
A word that rhymes with *pardon* Is where plants grow, in the _____.	garden
A word that rhymes with *inspire* Means to go to sleep, to _____.	retire
A word that rhymes with *repaired* Means to be frightened, to be _____.	scared

40

Rhyme	Word
A word that rhymes with *cease* Describes an oil product called _____.	grease
A word that rhymes with *mumble* Means lowly, unassuming, or _____.	humble
A word that rhymes with *curdle* Means to get across, or to _____.	hurdle
A word that rhymes with *rattle* Names a group of animals, it is _____.	cattle
A word that rhymes with *limber* Is another word for logs; it is _____.	timber
A word that rhymes with *care* Means to mend, or to _____.	repair
A word that rhymes with *wiper* Is an article of clothing for baby, the _____.	diaper
A word that rhymes with *date* Means cargo; it is _____.	freight
A word that rhymes with *repair* Means to make ready, or _____.	prepare
A word that rhymes with *fed* Means in place of, or _____.	instead
A word that rhymes with *keeper* Is a person not awake, a _____.	sleeper
A word that rhymes with *bleaker* Is a person who talks, a _____.	speaker
A word that rhymes with *clown* Is a part of speech, the _____.	pronoun
A word that rhymes with *insane* Means to make clear, or to _____.	explain
A word that rhymes with *feeling* Is the top of a room, the _____.	ceiling
A word that rhymes with *range* Means to be odd, to be _____.	strange
A word that rhymes with *simmer* Means to shine, or to _____.	glimmer
A word that rhymes with *buckle* Is a part of the finger, a _____.	knuckle

Cross rhymes

Explain that in this game, two definitions will be given. The words that match the definition will rhyme and will have the same middle letter.

The game may be conducted verbally by saying: "A word meaning (give definition) rhymes with a word meaning (give definition)." Draw a cross on the chalkboard and write in the words as the student supplies them.

Dittoed worksheets can be set up with the definitions to the left of the page and answer spaces in the form of a cross for each pair of definitions on the right of the page.

Definition	*Word*
an animal kept in the home	pet
still; remaining	yet

Definition	Word
to decay	rot
obtained	got
An enemy	foe
to plant seed	sow
two thousand pounds	ton
male child	son
rodent	rat
was seated; not standing	sat
flowed; moved quickly	ran
a container; is able	can
negative word	not
obtained	got
Is able; container	can
method of stirring the air	fan
storage place	bin
wrongdoing; evil	sin
black substance	tar
method of transportation	car
to scratch; deface	mar
distant	far
enjoyment; pleasure	fun
solar body	sun
part of a fish	fin
relative	kin
bread for hamburger sandwich	bun
firearm	gun
used eyes; had seen	saw
rule; the legal profession	law
evil; not good	bad
unhappy; sorrowful	sad
hole in the ground	pit
strike	hit
to exchange	trade
to mark; to rate	grade
direction	south
part of the face	mouth

Definition	*Word*
not at any time	never
means of lifting or turning	lever
huge; big	large
flat boat, usually towed	barge
vision	sight
opposite of day	night
to cut	sever
not at any time	never
to copy	trace
to make sturdy	brace
less than	fewer
not as old	newer
to take hold of	catch
what an egg sometimes does	hatch
article of clothing for woman	dress
lock of hair	tress
tone; to throw a ball	pitch
tie up (as a horse)	hitch
grow larger	swell
live in	dwell
conflict; battle	fight
not heavy	light
smallest amount	least
used to make dough rise	yeast
to rent	lease
halt; stop	cease
to welcome	greet
unexpected surprise; provide with free food	treat
to frighten	scare
warning device, usually used at night	flare

Word squares

The object of this game is to supply the three (four or five) words that match the definitions. The words must form a square and must be arranged so that the first and last letters of each word become the first and/or the last letter of another word.

Although the game may be played orally using the chalkboard, it works more successfully as a dittoed assignment. After giving general directions at the top of the page, group the definitions by threes, fours, or fives on the lefthand side. For each group of definitions, have an answer square off to the right.

Definition: _____

Definition: _____

Definition: _____

Definition	Word			Definition	Word		
tap lightly	p	a	t	is able	c	a	n
household animal	e		h	automobile	a		o
to bind	t	i	e	decay	r	o	t
an article				negative word			
enemy	f	o	e	eaten; devoured	a	t	e
stir the air	a		a	past	g		l
negative word	n	o	t	little person	o	f	f
devour				not on			

Definition	Word			Definition	Word		
atmosphere; opposite	s	k	y	male offspring	s	o	n
of earth	a		e	title of respect	i		u
sorrowful	d	o	t	almond, pecan, etc.	r	o	t
small speck				decay			
up to now; still							
plural pronoun	o		r	exist	a		e
a grain	a		a	feel ill	i		w
light brown	t	a	n	female sheep	l	i	e
sped				prone; fib			
to place	s		t	distant	f	a	r
observe	e		a	stir the air	a		e
organ of hearing	e	a	r	a primary color	n	o	d
black substance				bow			
obtained	g		t	walk quickly	r	u	n
fuel for automobile	a		a	remnant of cloth	a		u
to dip in the middle	s	a	g	almond, pecan, etc.	g	o	t
label; a game				obtained			
get larger	g	r	o	w	adore	l	o	v	e
equipment; outfit	e			e	earth; ground; alight	a			a
back	a			a	impression	n			s
erode; put on	r	e	a	r	a direction	d	e	n	t
place to sit	s	e	a	t	past; departed	g	o	n	e
put into storage	t			e	adhesive	l			a
a direction	o			s	merit; deserve	u			r
examination	w	e	s	t	smooth,	e	v	e	n
				opposite of odd				
gone by	p	a	s	t	part of face	n	o	s	e
opening in skin	o			o	by; close to	e			a
comfort	r			r	hurry	a			c
ripped	e	a	s	e	every	r	u	s	h
wet weather	r	a	i	n	discover	f	i	n	d
wooden flat boat	a			o	not succeed	a			e
story	f			t	following all the rest	i			n
short letter	t	a	l	e	impression	l	a	s	t
sketch; attract	d	r	a	w	to separate, classify	s	o	r	t
past tense of draw	r			e	not hard	o			a
growth on body	e			s	relate	f			i
a direction	w	a	r	t	appendage on animal	t	e	l	l

Definition	*Word*	*Definition*	*Word*
legend; story	l o r e	a color	g r a y
type of soil	o a	take hold of	r e
many; great deal	a c	twelve months	a a
every	m u c h	grizzly animal	b e a r
unit of weight	o u n c e	smallest amount	l e a s t
fish-eating animal	t v	not the winner	o h
send in	t e	to lift higher	s r
(as payment)	e n	a number	e e
happening	r e m i t		r a i s e
blame	f a u l t	a direction	s o u t h
belief	a e	change position	h o
tie up	i a	pairs	i u
instruct	t c	units of time	f r
	h i t c h		t w i n s
deserve, virtue	m e r i t	task	c h o r e
coins, currency	o o	place to sit	h v
younger years	n u	cut of meat	a e
feel	e c	happening	i n
	y o u t h		r o a s t
leaving; departing	g o i n g	last; not to be	f i n a l
big; wonderful	r o	changed	i a
thick	a o	before all others	r d
large water bird	n s	that place	s l
	d e n s e	long-handled	t h e r e
		spoon	
subtract	m i n u s	a direction	n o r t h
part of face	o t	opposite of day	i e
employed;	u a	not loose	g a
signed on	t n	part of body	h r
be erect	h i r e d		t i g h t
circular	r o u n d	large; wonderful	g r a d e
type of race	e i	to rate	r a
early years	l t	one who keeps	e g
narrow trench;	a c	time	a e
to get rid of	y o u t h	enthusiastic	t i m e r

Sound-alikes

Explain that some words sound alike but are spelled differently and have different meanings (*to, too, two*). These words are called *homophones*. Tell the children that in this game, the object is to supply the homophones from the given definitions.

After introducing the game in this manner, you may want to play the game verbally or to ditto game sheets for seatwork. The following directions are useful if the game is played orally: "A word meaning (give definition) sounds the same as a word meaning (give definition)." The game sheets can be set up in the same way as the lists below, substituting a blank for the homophones.

Definition	*Homophone*
had eaten; devoured	ate
a number	eight
an antlered animal	deer
precious; adored	dear
to have expelled air	blew
a primary color	blue
a personal pronoun	you
female sheep	ewe

Definition	*Homophone*
to spread seed	sow
to stitch	sew
vision	sight
a place	site
interested; spellbound	rapt
knocked; talked	rapped
ashen; weak in color	pale
a container; bucket	pail
also; and	too
a number; pair	two
male child	son
celestial body	sun
not old	new
understand; had the answer	knew
rain, sunshine, etc.	weather
. . . or not	whether
appear to be	seem
where two pieces of material meet	seam
a royal person	knight
opposite of day	night
united part of two pieces of rope	knot
negative word	not
to travel on water	sail
merchandise at reduced price	sale
an aroma; odor	scent
one penny	cent
to purchase	buy
near; past	by
structure over a fence	stile
fashion	style
to rasp; metal protection over opening	grate
big; wonderful	great
timber	wood
willing to do	would
was victorious	won
a unit	one

Definition	*Homophone*
to snap	break
part used for stopping (as a car)	brake
a female relative	aunt
small insect	ant
stinging insect	bee
exist	be
person who pays to live in someone's house	boarder
edge; rim	border
an accomplishment	feat
parts of the lower body	feet
to cure	heal
part of the foot	heel
understand	know
negative word	no
a froglike creature	toad
having toes	toed
guided	led
a metal	lead
small particle	mote
ditch around a castle	moat
understands; has knowledge of	knows
part of the face	nose
a positive answer; affirmative vote	aye
organ of sight	eye
a preposition	in
small hotel	inn
narrow passageway	lane
put into horizontal position	lain
ordinary; unadorned	plain
surface	plane
a fruit	pear
two that match	pair
the ocean	sea
understand; use eyes	see
sighted; noticed	seen
part of a play; where something takes place	scene

50

Definition	Homophone
tumble; move smoothly; a pastry	roll
an actor's part	role
type of weather	rain
to rule	reign
a story	tale
on the end of an animal	tail
a spool (as for fishing)	reel
true; actual	real
used to guide horses	rein
to rule	reign
method; direction	way
measure pounds, ounces, etc.	weigh
measurement	weight
stay in place; hesitate	wait
frozen rain	hail
healthy; hearty	hale
a hollow space	hole
entire	whole
to moan or groan loudly	wail
a large mammal	whale
a blood vessel	vein
conceited; stuck-up	vain
a glen; spot in the forest	vale
cloth worn over hat and face	veil
masculine	male
postal service	mail
either	or
native metal	ore
unit of time	hour
plural pronoun	our
to have ridden	rode
a street	road
by way of	through
tossed	threw
in favor of; a preposition	for
a number	four

51

Definition	Homophone
a rabbit	hare
what grows on the head	hair
honest	fair
price of a ride, food	fare
one who inherits	heir
what we breathe	air
belonging to them	their
that place	there
to listen; heed	hear
this place	here
to fly	soar
ache; hurt; injury	sore
to drill	bore
male pig	boar
a color	red
what was done to a book	read
only; part of a shoe	sole
intangible part of man	soul
long, slender grass	reed
what you do with a book	read
to take advantage of	prey
to ask for help, guidance, etc.	pray
to take a vote (such as opinions)	poll
a long stick	pole
single	lone
opposite of to borrow	loan
to encounter or join	meet
a kind of food	meat

Double meanings

Explain that some words are spelled and pronounced alike but have two or more completely different meanings. These words are called *homonyms*.

The object of this game is to supply the one word that matches both definitions. The game may be played orally or used for seatwork.

Definition	*Homonym*
is allowed; a month	may
part of a play; to do	act
parcel of ground; large quantity	lot
faucet; touch lightly	tap
article of men's clothing; bind	tie
emotional outburst; suitable	fit
is able; tin container	can
part of race; to drink, as a dog	lap
to mimic; an animal	ape
to operate (as machine); move forward hurriedly	run
household animal; caress	pet
hole; stone of fruit	pit
to mail; part of a fence	post
attract; sketch	draw
to beat; article for encouraging a horse	whip

Definition	Homonym
obey; part of person that feels, thinks, etc.	mind
close tightly; a mammal	seal
without heat; a common sickness	cold
run quickly; small arrow	dart
an act; legal document	deed
cut into squares; a square object	cube
specific time; a fruit of the palm	date
dunce; victimize	fool
part of lower body; unit of measure	foot
bad-tempered person; tool for starting engine	crank
top of head; object worn by royalty	crown
to throw; musical tone	pitch
piece of furniture; list of information	table
hobo; walk heavily	tramp
to protect; position on football team	guard
telegram; a strong rope	cable
ornate; to imagine	fancy
group of ships; swift in motion	fleet
to make unclear; formation in sky	cloud
term of affection; product from bees	honey
serious; where people are buried	grave
vegetable; crush	squash
season of year; shoot forth	spring
part of mouth; handle on wagon	tongue
to pound; carpenter's tool	hammer
fishing gear; position on football team	tackle
rectangle with equal sides; an open area	square
to mimic; bright-colored bird	parrot
group of fish; place to learn	school
twist; a tool for turning	wrench
gentle; easily damaged, soft	tender
alter; money in small denominations	change
portion of time; sentence ending	period

Hidden words (categories)

The idea of this game is to find a word that matches the definition given and that contains another word belonging to the correct category. First, tell the student the category, e.g., animals. Next, give him a definition and ask him to supply the word that matches it. Finally, have him find the animal hidden within the word. If there is no animal in the word, he has made a mistake and must correct his original word. You might wish to word your instructions something like this: "The category is _____. A word meaning (give definition) contains another word that is a (give category). The first word is _____. The (give category) it contains is _____."

Once the students understand how to play the game, it may be used for seatwork by setting up the game sheets in the same way as the word lists that follow. Put blanks in place of the words and include some general instructions at the top of the page.

Definition	Word	Category Word
CATEGORY: PARTS OF BODY		
large scissors	shears	ear
to adore	worship	hip
obscure one orb by another	eclipse	lip

55

Definition	Word	Category Word

Category: Parts of Body — *continued*

Definition	Word	Category Word
to attain knowledge	learn	ear
place where crops are grown	farm	arm
to write carelessly	scribble	rib
a fine drawing	etching	chin
to mar; scratch	deface	face
according to law	legal	leg
to bow down, as in church	kneel	knee
to touch; used for holding	handle	hand
bad mistake; goof	boner	bone

Category: Numbers

Definition	Word	Category Word
seat for royalty	throne	one
devoured; has dined	eaten	ten
cargo ship	freighter	eight
instrument for communication	telephone	one
currency	money	one
ounces, pounds, etc.	weight	eight
gentle; easily damaged; soft	tender	ten
skeleton part	bone	one
to secure; pin	fasten	ten
what bees make	honey	one
degree; range or distance	extent	ten

Category: Pronouns

Definition	Word	Category Word
a small building	shed	she/he
that place	there	her
used in sewing to protect finger	thimble	him
to talk about	discuss	us
arrived	came	me
a trip	journey	our
early part of life	youth	you
departed	went	we
national song	anthem	them
a foe	enemy	my
a metal used in cans	tin	I
listen; heed	hear	he

Category: Birds and Insects

Definition	Word	Category Word
sound made by dog	growl	owl
that time	then	hen

56

Definition	Word	Category Word

CATEGORY: BIRDS AND INSECTS — *continued*

Definition	Word	Category Word
cowardly	craven	raven
frown; look angry	scowl	owl
to seed	plant	ant
kind of small dog	beagle	eagle
female parent	mother	moth
to draw near	approach	roach
tool for turning	wrench	wren
what a king wears	crown	crow
an insect having hard outer wings	beetle	bee
not straight; leans to the side	slants	ant

CATEGORY: ANIMALS

Definition	Word	Category Word
form	shape	ape
hair on face	beard	bear
to take hold of	catch	cat
a sly kind of animal	fox	ox
clothing for a baby	diaper	ape
person who does something	doer	doe
less than	fewer	ewe
person who is afraid	coward	cow
rules of a language	grammar	ram
faucet	spigot	pig
portion; to divide up	share	hare

CATEGORY: WEATHER

Definition	Word	Category Word
dishonest; play unfairly	cheat	heat
bawled out; corrected sharply	scolded	cold
mode of transportation	train	rain
fired a gun	shot	hot
hole in wall covered with glass	window	wind
hold back; don't do	refrain	rain
group of bees or insects	swarm	warm
person who expects the best	optimist	mist
part of body; helps you think	brain	rain
entertain royally	regale	gale

CATEGORY: WEIGHTS AND MEASURES

Definition	Word	Category Word
expression of happiness on face	smile	mile
to jump upon	pounce	ounce

Definition	Word	Category Word
CATEGORY: WEIGHTS AND MEASURES *—continued*		
to squeeze between finger and thumb	pinch	inch
part of mouth	tongue	ton
small river	stream	ream
to goad	prod	rod
plot; plan; chart	diagram	gram
small dot	speck	peck
type of bird	finch	inch
line through center	diameter	meter
speak out	expound	pound
make sure; grasp securely	clinch	inch
CATEGORY: TREES		
animal covered with stiff bristles	porcupine	pine
sound a frog makes	croak	oak
shoot a gun; blaze	fire	fir
cut; long rip	slash	ash
lance; long sword	spear	pear
feather	plume	plum
body form; a written number	figure	fig
wrestle with	grapple	apple
used to steer ship	helm	elm
to let stand in water	soak	oak
go out of sight	disappear	pear

Hidden words (opposites)

In this game, definitions are given for two words. Hidden within each of these words is another word; these two hidden words are opposites. The student has two goals: to supply the word that matches each definition, and to identify the opposites in each pair of words.

When playing the game orally, be sure to write the words on the chalkboard as the children supply them. It will be easier for them to pick out the opposites if they can see the words written down rather than having to visualize them.

Here are sample directions to use on dittoed game sheets or when playing the game orally: "You will guess two words from the two definitions given below (I will give you). In each of these words there is a shorter word. The two hidden words in each pair are opposites—for example, *hot* and *cold*, or *off* and *on*."

Definition	Word	Definition	Word	Opposites
fired a gun	shot	to correct someone sharply	scold	hot–cold
to sneer	scoff	single; by oneself	alone	off–on
to start	begin	to yell	shout	in–out
male parent	father	an object	thing	fat–thin
keep; maintain	hold	a child	youngster	old–young
a Roman fighter	gladiator	worn by a horse	saddle	glad–sad
to put in a bank	deposit	comprehend	understand	sit–stand
grow larger	swell	not succeeding	failing	well–ailing
a hole (as window)	opening	storage place	closet	open–close
related; narrated	told	understood; was aware	knew	old–new
black or green fruit	olive	did lessons	studied	live–die
trip by air	flight	deprive of light	darken	light–dark
evening meal	supper	a heavy rain	downpour	up–down
feeling of self-respect	pride	cement path	sidewalk	ride–walk
to permit	allow	part of the leg	thigh	low–high
lid	cover	sound following lightning	thunder	over–under
fate	destiny	intolerant of others' beliefs	bigoted	tiny–big
food for animals	fodder	a number	seven	odd–even
salary; money received	income	horned animal	goat	come–go
a split	cleft	to scare	frighten	left–right
oily	greasy	green vegetable	chard	easy–hard
male royalty	knight	this time period	today	night–day
worn on hands	gloves	no matter what	whatever	love–hate
a day of the week	Saturday	resisted successfully	withstood	sat–stood
unexpected event	surprise	cascading water	waterfall	rise–fall
a chore	task	of the stars	stellar	ask–tell
to pardon; to excuse	forgive	wooden support	stake	give–take

Add-a-prefix

In this game, two definitions and a prefix are given. The object is first to identify the four-letter word that matches the first definition and then to make a new word by adding the prefix. The new word must match the second definition.

Definition	Word	Definition	Word
PREFIX: COM			
sit for a portrait	pose	create (as music)	compose
heap	pile	collect material for a volume	compile
to peel	pare	measure against another	compare
to go by	pass	instrument telling direction	compass
speechless	mute	change; convert	commute
treaty	pact	concentrated in small area	compact
fortified place	fort	ease; consolation	comfort
repair	mend	recommend as worthy	commend
PREFIX: CON			
hole in the earth	cave	hollowed, as a bowl	concave
pipe; channel; tube	duct	escort; guide	conduct
solid; a business	firm	acknowledge; prove truth of	confirm
shape	form	adapt; act as majority does	conform
device to set off bomb	fuse	perplex; mix up	confuse

Definition	Word	Definition	Word

PREFIX: CON—*continued*

Definition	Word	Definition	Word
dispatched	sent	agreement; give approval	consent
part of shoe; lone	sole	give comfort to	console
yield by treaty	cede	admit; give in	concede
finished	done	pardon; overlook; excuse	condone
very good	fine	restrict	confine
short letter	note	associate with	connote
examination	test	race; competition	contest

PREFIX: IN

Definition	Word	Definition	Word
has one's senses	sane	mad; irrational	insane
escape passage; outlet for air, smoke, etc.	vent	create; devise	invent
group that judges	jury	wound	injury
hearty; healthy	hale	draw in (as air)	inhale
impression	dent	space in from margin	indent
shape	form	teach; give information to	inform
solid; a business	firm	weak of mind or body	infirm
religious denomination	sect	small animal; bug	insect
care for	tend	mean; have purpose	intend
canvas house	tent	concentrated; purpose	intent
church steeple	spire	influence	inspire
fee paid to college	tuition	quick insight	intuition

PREFIX: IM

Definition	Word	Definition	Word
treaty	pact	effect; forceful collision	impact
two of a kind	pair	damage; injure	impair
unmixed with anything else	pure	not clean	impure
ashen	pale	pierce; enclose with stakes	impale
portion; separate	part	give from one's own store	impart
harbor town	port	bring from another country	import
sit for a portrait	pose	force upon	impose

PREFIX: AD

Definition	Word	Definition	Word
outlet for air, smoke, etc.	vent	coming; arrival	advent
this place	here	stick to	adhere
unite	join	lie next to	adjoin
part of speech; shows action	verb	part of speech; modifies	adverb

Definition	Word	Definition	Word
PREFIX: PRE			
peel (as fruit)	pare	make ready	prepare
yield by treaty	cede	come before	precede
outlet for air, smoke, etc.	vent	keep from happening	prevent
dispatched	sent	gift; in attendance	present
lateral section	side	act as chairman	preside
care for	tend	make believe	pretend
confront; part of head	face	introductory statement in book	preface
tardy	late	church official	prelate
wise man; seasoning	sage	foreshadow; omen	presage
school book	text	alleged motive	pretext
be of use	serve	protect or maintain	preserve
PREFIX: UN			
has ability	able	incapable	unable
related; narrated	told	too many to count; kept secret	untold
twist	bend	straighten	unbend
carnival; honest	fair	not just	unfair
fewer than	less	except	unless
sleep; relaxation	rest	turmoil; disturbed state	unrest
past tense of see	seen	invisible; not visible	unseen
simple; not difficult	easy	worried; restless	uneasy
PREFIX: AP			
in abeyance; to wait	pend	to add to	append
a fruit	pear	seem; come into view	appear
to make dull or unpleasant	pall	dismay	appall
sound of a bell	peal	entreaty; plea	appeal
PREFIX: EN			
bring together; unite	join	order or command	enjoin
sing	chant	bewitch	enchant
a series of links	chain	bind or hold	enchain
bring legal action against	sue	follow	ensue
wealthy	rich	make more valuable	enrich
tumble; pastry	roll	register (as for class)	enroll
part of auto wheel	tire	all	entire

Definition	Word	Definition	Word
PREFIX: RE			
to quote	cite	repeat from memory	recite
heavy string	cord	set down in writing	record
shape	form	correct; make again	reform
unite	join	answer; unite again	rejoin
tardy	late	tell; narrate	relate
chief; most important	main	stay	remain
sign; grade	mark	comment	remark
small particle	mote	distant; secluded	remote
transfer; make motion	move	change location; dismiss	remove
two of a kind	pair	mend	repair
gone by	past	a meal	repast
sit for portrait	pose	lie at rest; a state of rest	repose
dispatched; mailed	sent	feel displeasure against	resent
lateral surface	side	live in	reside
omen; poster	sign	quit	resign
separate	sort	vacation spot; look for help	resort
meat of a calf	veal	expose; show	reveal

Word plus

In this game, the student must supply three words from the definitions he is given. If he chooses the first two words correctly, they will combine to make the third word, which must also match the given definition. Be sure to tell the students that the new word may not be pronounced exactly like the two short words (e.g., *don* and *or* — *donor*).

Use the following instructions for a dittoed assignment or for playing the game orally. "A word meaning (give definition) can be joined with a word meaning (give definition) to make a word that means (give definition)."

Definition	Word	Definition	Word	Definition	Word
personal pronoun	me	an article	an	intend; viscious	mean
into higher position	up	preposition; touching	on	above; over	upon
personal pronoun	me	preposition	at	kind of food	meat
thus	so	preposition	on	not long from now	soon
thus	so	fourth note on scale	fa	couch	sofa
masculine pronoun	he	advertisement	ad	part of the body	head
start; leave	go	preposition	at	an animal	goat
masculine pronoun	he	preposition	at	warmth	heat
thus	so	into higher position	up	liquid food	soup
preposition; about	of	a number	ten	frequent	often
a preposition	to	twenty-four hours	day	this time period	today
negative word	no	angry; insane	mad	wanderer	nomad
masculine pronoun	he	talent; drawing	art	part of body	heart
plural pronoun	us	time period	age	purpose	usage
personal pronoun	me	small insect	ant	intended	meant
thus	so	cover	lid	not liquid	solid
masculine pronoun	he	marry	wed	cut; chopped	hewed
exists	is	take to court	sue	come forth	issue
like; while	as	speak; utter	say	examine ore	assay
exist	am	utilize; purpose	use	entertain	amuse
exists	is	earth	land	land surrounded by water	island
preposition	in	calm; sensible	sane	mad	insane
plural pronoun	we	sin; bad	evil	small bettle	weevil
preposition	to	fend off; protect	ward	going to	toward
exist	be	possess	have	act; obey	behave

do	accomplish	sage	wise; seasoning	dosage	amount
be	exist	hold	keep; maintain	behold	see; understand
in	preposition	come	arrive	income	money earned
be	exist	ware	article for sale	beware	take heed
in	preposition	tend	take care of	intend	mean; purpose
as	like; while	cent	a penny	ascent	act of rising
pa	slang for father	rent	hire; lease	parent	mother or father
me	personal pronoun	dial	part of watch	medial	middle
fa	fourth note of scale	mine	belongs to me	famine	starvation
may	can; permitted to	be	to exist	maybe	perhaps
cab	taxi	in	preposition	cabin	small house
elf	small creature; fairy	in	preposition	elfin	like an elf
may	can; permitted to	or	either	mayor	head of city government
mad	angry; insane	am	part of "to be"	madam	title for lady
car	automobile	at	preposition	carat	size (as gems)
man	male person	or	either	manor	large home
beg	to plea	in	preposition	begin	start
dog	household pet	ma	slang for mother	dogma	established opinions
don	to put on	or	either	donor	one who gives
ray	beam of light	on	opposite of off	rayon	kind of material
fur	pelt of animal	or	either	furor	frenzy; rage
car	automobile	rot	decay	carrot	orange-colored vegetable
but	except	ton	two thousand pounds	button	clothes fastener
for	in favor of	get	obtain	forget	not remember

Definition	Word	Definition	Word	Word	Definition
a skillet	pan	attempt	try	pantry	storage place
automobile	car	trained animal	pet	carpet	rug
negative word	not	had eaten	ate	notate	make note
overweight	fat	feminine person	her	father	parent
negative word	not	frozen water	ice	notice	take heed
to slice	cut	allow	let	cutlet	slice of meat
encountered	met	cement carrier	hod	method	way; manner
ocean	sea	male	man	seaman	sailor
equal	par	put on	don	pardon	forgive
black substance	tar	obtain	get	target	goal
to deface; scratch	mar	metal; can	tin	martin	small bird
short sleep	nap	related	kin	napkin	protective cloth
final	end	organ of hearing	ear	endear	make beloved
not thin	fat	a number	ten	fatten	make fleshy
block (as water)	dam	period of time	age	damage	harm; wreck
small insect	ant	border of dress	hem	anthem	national song
rodent	rat	feminine pronoun	her	rather	preferably
was seated	sat	anger	ire	satire	ridicule
to deface; scratch	mar	ruler of country	king	marking	writing on
organ of hearing	ear	home for birds	nest	earnest	sincere
hastened; sped	ran	a bag	sack	ransack	search
hair on animal	fur	opposite of short	long	furlong	220 yards
feminine pronoun	her	to peal	ring	herring	kind of fish
worn on head	cap	can do	able	capable	has ability
armed conflict	war	food; cost of ride	fare	warfare	military operation
Hawaiian garland	lei	certain	sure	leisure	idle time
organ of hearing	ear	at that time	then	earthen	of the earth

in favor of	for	song; melody	tune	wealth; fate	fortune
sped; walked fast	ran	male royalty	king	high position	ranking
short line	bar	to win; earn	gain	sale; haggle	bargain
equal	par	can do	able	story with moral	parable
light tap	pat	kind of water bird	tern	model	pattern
small demon	imp	every	each	vote out of office	impeach
kind of meat	ham	ridicule	mock	swinging bed	hammock

(*Note*: The following are not categorized by size and include some more complex words.)

exist	be	not as tame	wilder	confuse	bewilder
lower part	base	round toy	ball	game	baseball
slender	thin	male royalty	king	using brain	thinking
earth	sod	an article	a	soft drink	soda
mail; fence part	post	period of time	age	fee for mail	postage
harbor town	port	beam of light	ray	make picture of	portray
a fruit	plum	period of time	age	feathers	plumage
plot; design	plan	male royalty	king	wide, heavy floor boards	planking
capsule (medical)	pill	period of time	age	loot; ransack	pillage
part of body	neck	meshed fabric	lace	beads	necklace
small rug	mat	lock of hair	tress	cushion	mattress
cost of ride	fare	not sick	well	goodbye	farewell
passageway	hall	was in debt	owed	sacred	hallowed
musical group	band	period of time	age	wound covering	bandage
gone by	past	either	or	clergyman	pastor
a very light rain	mist	corrosion	rust	lack of confidence	mistrust
go by	pass	period of time	age	hallway	passage
conclusion	end	fury	anger	to put into danger	endanger
banner; pennant	flag	rave	rant	glaring	flagrant

Define and combine

This game is the same as "Word plus" except that three words (instead of two) are combined to form a new word. Explain this to the players and give them the definition of the longer word first. Tell them that the word that matches this definition can be broken down into three smaller words. Then read the definitions of the three smaller words. You might want to point out that the longer word will not necessarily sound like the three shorter words put together.

When this game is played orally, write the words on the chalkboard as the students supply them. (The game will probably be too difficult if they have to visualize the words.) If the game is used as a dittoed assignment, you may wish to set up the game sheet like the word lists that follow, substituting blanks for the words.

A word that means the act of being at a place is **attendance.**

a preposition	at
a number	ten
move to music	dance

A word that means a group of travelers, as on a desert is **caravan.**

an automobile	car
an article	a
moving truck	van

70

A word that means a sweater that is open down the
front is   **cardigan.**

automobile	car
remove earth	dig
an article	an

A word that means the act (or trade) of building is   **carpentry.**

automobile	car
enclosure for animals	pen
attempt	try

A word that means to punish severely is   **castigate.**

to throw out a fishing line;

actors in a play	cast
personal pronoun	I
opening in a fence	gate

A word that means to list or to enumerate is   **catalog.**

household pet	cat
an article	a
piece of a tree	log

A word that means a measure of length is   **centimeter**

a penny	cent
personal pronoun	I
measurer; unit of length	meter

A word that means a large fire is   **conflagration**

negative position; opposite of

pro	con
banner; symbol of nation or state	flag
a fixed amount of food, gas, etc.	ration

A word that means the opening that a door closes is   **doorway**

accomplish; act	do
either	or
method; route	way

A word that means a large, winged insect is   **dragonfly**

to tow; pull along behind	drag
aboard	on
to soar	fly

A word that means a body of people entitled to
vote is **electorate.**

chose by vote	elect
either	, or
devoured	ate

A word that means to leave out of a sentence is **ellipsis**

short for raised train	el
part of the mouth	lip
slang for female relative	sis

A word that means to whip or lash is **flagellate.**

banner; symbol of nation or state	flag
short for raised train	el
tardy	late

A word that means an ancestor is **forefather.**

front; forward; before	fore
overweight	fat
feminine pronoun	her

A word that means likely to be forgotten is **forgettable.**

in favor of	for
obtain	get
piece of furniture	table

A word that means exceptional, powerful, or feared is **formidable.**

in favor of	for
the part in the middle	mid
can do	able

A word that means machine that converts one type
of energy into another is **generator.**

hereditary element	gene
rodent	rat
either	or

A word that means the largest of the anthropoid
apes is **gorilla.**

to depart; leave	go
small brook	rill
an article	a

A word that means a trade requiring the skilled
use of one's hands is   **handicraft.**

    the part of the arm used for
    grasping   hand
    personal pronoun   I
    skill; a trade   craft

A word that means sorrow is   **heartache.**

    masculine pronoun   he
    talent; drawing   art
    pain   ache

A word that means uncivilized is   **heathen.**

    masculine pronoun   he
    a conjunction   at
    female chicken   hen

A word that means half of the earth is   **hemisphere.**

    border of a dress   hem
    personal pronoun   I
    an orb   . sphere

A word that means birthright, legacy, tradition is   **heritage.**

    feminine pronoun   her
    that thing   it
    period of time   age

A word that means unlikely is   **improbable.**

    small demon   imp
    to steal   rob
    can do   able

A word that means beyond healing is   **incurable.**

    opposite of out   in
    mongrel dog   cur
    adept   able

A word that means anger at something that is un-
just is   **indignation.**

    opposite of out   in
    remove earth   dig
    federation of states   nation

A word that means childlike is   **infantile.**

opposite of out	in
stir the air	fan
piece of fired clay used for floors or roofs	tile

A word that means soldiers trained to fight on foot is   **infantry.**

opposite of out	in
stir the air	fan
attempt	try

A word that means one who gives information is   **informant.**

opposite of out	in
shape	form
a small insect	ant

A word that means unfairness to another is   **injustice.**

opposite of out	in
honest, fair	just
frozen water	ice

A word that means intolerable is   **insufferable.**

opposite of out	in
feel pain	suffer
can do; adept	able

A word that means to nullify is   **invalidate.**

opposite of out	in
sound; effective; true	valid
devoured	ate

A word that means to quarantine or set apart is   **isolate.**

personal pronoun	I
thus	so
tardy	late

A word that means keen, well-versed is   **knowledgeable.**

understand; aware of	know
a shelf	ledge
adept; can do	able

A word that means deplorable, regrettable is   **lamentable.**

note of the scale	la
males	men
article of furniture	table

74

A word that means to make by joining layers is **laminate.**

flee hastily	lam
opposite of out	in
devoured	ate

A word that means an army officer is **lieutenant.**

in place of	lieu
a number	ten
small insect	ant

A word that means to dispute, carry on a lawsuit, or a contest in law is **litigate.**

illuminated, to have set fire to	lit
personal pronoun	I
opening in fence	gate

A word that means a kind of wood is **mahogany.**

slang for mother	ma
swine	hog
one taken at random	any

A word that means capable of being controlled is **manageable.**

masculine person	man
period of time	age
adapt	able

A word that means trim and polish fingernails is **manicure.**

a male	man
personal pronoun	I
heal	cure

A word that means of or relating to navigation or commerce at sea is **maritime.**

to deface	mar
personal pronoun	I
hours, minutes, etc.	time

A word that means a daytime performance is **matinee.**

small rug	mat
personal pronoun	I
born	nee

A word that means remarkable, outstanding, or conspicuous is **noticeable.**

negative word	not
frozen water	ice
adept	able

75

A word that means to compose for an instrumental
group is   **orchestrate.**
either	or
part of upper body	chest
grade	rate

A word that means source or ancestry is   **origin.**
either	or
personal pronoun	I
where cotton is separated	gin

A word that means loose-fitting nightwear is   **pajamas.**
slang for father	pa
jelly	jam
like; while	as

A word that means bold cliffs or a fence of stakes
for defense is   **palisade.**
friend; buddy	pal
exists	is
fruit drink	ade

A word that means throb or beat rapidly is   **palpitate.**
friend; buddy	pal
hole in ground	pit
devoured	ate

A word that means to perform without words is   **pantomime.**
a kettle or pot	pan
preposition	to
mimic	mime

A word that means a group of words beginning
with an indented line   **paragraph.**
equal	par
an article	a
a table; list of data	graph

A word that means an organism that lives in or on
another is   **parasite.**
equal	par
an article	a
place; location	site

New from Fearon

TEACHER AIDS

Arts & Crafts
Draw Your Own Zoo and Color It Too
Planning and Producing Slides and Filmstrips for the
Classroom

Classroom Activities
Classroom Learning Centers
Designing Classroom Simulations
Ideas for Learning Centers
Word Puzzles

Early Childhood Education
Focusing on the Strengths of Children
Free and Inexpensive Materials for Pre-school and
Early Childhood
Nursery School Bulletin Boards

General Interest
Classroom Behavior from A to Z
The Teacher's Survival Guide
Writing and Evaluating Curriculum Guides

Social Studies & Science
Enriched Social Studies Teaching: Through the Use
of Games and Activities
Science Games for the Elementary School

Language Arts
Choral Speaking
Games Make Spelling Fun, rev.
Independent Language Arts Activities: Seatwork for
the Primary Grades
Independent Language Arts Activities: Practice and
Enrichment for the Intermediate Grades
Library Skills
Listening and Learning: Practical Activities for De-
veloping Listening Skills
100 Individualized Activities for Reading
77 Games for Reading Groups
Teach Yourself i.t.a.
Telling Stories through Movement

Fearon Bulletin Board Series

Americans-All	Men and Women of the World
American History	Music
Careers	Other Peoples—Other Lands
Community Helpers	Poetry and Literature
Consumer Education	Reading and Writing
Environment	Science
Government	Spelling and Phonics
Health and Safety	Sports
Language Mechanics	Values and Morals
Mathematics	World History

PROFESSIONAL LIBRARY

Early Childhood
Classroom Management and Behavioral Objectives
(Piper)
40 Innovative Programs in Early Childhood Education
(Fallon, ed.)

Materials for Classroom Management (Piper)
Nursery School Management Guide (Cherry et al.)

Innovative Education
Accountability for Teachers and School Administra-
tors (Ornstein, ed.)
Criterion-Referenced Instruction (Popham)
Curriculum Development (Gilchrist)
Developing a Systems View of Education (Banathy)

Educator's Fact Book on School Organization (Miller)
Measuring Instructional Intent (Mager)
Public Relations for Schools (Unruh & Willier)
Relevance and the Social Studies (Madgic)
The Uses of Instructional Objectives (Popham)

Send for a complete catalog

LEAR SIEGLER, INC./FEARON PUBLISHERS 6 Davis Drive, Belmont, California 94002

ISBN-0-8224-7485-9